First Published in the UK in 2019 by Focus Education (UK) Ltd

Focus Education (UK) Ltd
Publishing
Talking Point Conference & Exhibition Centre
Huddersfield Road
Scouthead
Saddleworth
OL4 4AG

Focus Education (UK) Ltd Reg. No 4507968

ISBN 978-1-911416-22-7

CW01652134

Companies, institutions and other organisations wishing to make bulk purchases of books published by Focus Education should contact their local bookstore or Focus Education direct:

Customer Services, Focus Education, Talking Point Conference & Exhibition Centre, Huddersfield Road, Scouthead, Saddleworth, OL4 4AG
Tel 01457 821818 Fax 01457 878205

www.focus-education.co.uk
customerservice@focus-education.co.uk
Printed in Great Britain by Focus Education UK Ltd, Scouthead

focuseducationuk

focuseducation1

focus-education-uk-ltd

ABOUT THE AUTHOR

Tim Nelson is an Associate Consultant with Focus Education. This role involves leading large scale national conferences, working with groups of schools, working with individual schools and inspecting schools. Tim regularly mentors trainee inspectors.

Prior to working with Focus Education he worked as a head teacher (until 2012). Tim's last school had a reputation for innovation and their initiatives have been utilised by others and presented internationally. He has a proven track record of impacting on school improvement. This has resulted in work as:

- a local leader of education
- a school improvement partner
- an Ofsted inspector
- a professional partner.

Tim is experienced at working with teams in school with a focus on all core areas of school improvement, i.e. curriculum assessment, teaching and learning, leadership and management etc.

Tim has written a wide range of publications. Some of Tim's most recent and best selling publications are:

- Moving Lessons to Good
- Designing Pre and Post Learning Challenges across the Curriculum
- RE Learning Challenge Curriculum
- Maths Learning Challenge Curriculum
- Music Learning Challenge Curriculum
- Design & Technology Learning Challenge Curriculum
- Art Learning Challenge Curriculum
- Enriching the Curriculum
- Judging Teaching, not the Teacher
- Judging Teaching in the Early Years, not the Early Years Teacher (co-authored with Sarah Quinn)
- Evaluating SMSC Development and the promotion of British Values

Contents

Bloom's Taxonomy of cognitive objectives was originally developed in the 1950s by Benjamin Bloom and revised by Anderson and Krathwohl.

This resource has been designed to support teachers in developing effective questioning based on these revisions and utilising the 'Knowledge Dimension' as it has been applied to each stage of the taxonomy.

Focusing on the acquisition of knowledge recognises the recent Ofsted emphasis that schools ensure pupils are taught knowledge, and skills, in all subjects.

The format also acknowledges metacognition as a proven way to rapidly improve pupils' learning and progress. The Education Endowment Foundation's 'Teaching and Learning Toolkit' states, "Metacognition and self-regulation approaches have consistently high levels of impact."

The questions in the subject sections of this book are designed as a starting point for adults and are provided as examples to be adapted by individual teachers and teaching assistants. Where applicable, the questions are based on the National Curriculum Programme of Study (2014).

Ideally, the pupils will also be involved in asking their own questions and developing an awareness of their own learning, following the principles of metacognition.

Using the subject resources

Bloom's revised taxonomy.

There are six levels of cognitive learning according to the revised version of Bloom's Taxonomy. Each level is conceptually different.

The six levels are:

- Remembering
- Understanding
- Applying
- Analyzing
- Evaluating
- Creating

For each of these levels, the subject resources in this book provide a set of example questions. These questions can be used as they are provided, or adapted for the specific knowledge being taught in that unit of work.

Research has shown that the majority of teachers' questions focus on the remember and understand levels of the taxonomy. Therefore, it is important to ensure that teachers provide a range of questions across all the levels.

Using the subject resources

The resources in this book are based on Bloom's revised taxonomy and also the knowledge dimension. The knowledge dimension represents a range from concrete (factual) to abstract (metacognitive), as shown below:

concrete knowledge ⟶			abstract knowledge
Factual	**Conceptual**	**Procedural**	**Metacognitive**
Knowledge of terminology Knowledge of specific details and elements	Knowledge of classifications and categories Knowledge of principles and generalisations Knowledge of theories and, models and structures	Knowledge of subject-specific skills, techniques and methods Knowledge of when to use appropriate procedures	Strategic knowledge Self-knowledge Knowledge about cognitive tasks including appropriate contextual and conditional knowledge.

Note: Representation of the knowledge dimension as a number of discrete steps can be a bit misleading. For example, all procedural knowledge may not be more abstract than all conceptual knowledge. However, it is useful for teachers to think about the type of knowledge the pupils are acquiring over time and to ensure that questioning includes the metacognitive stage.

Background information

Education inspection framework - Overview of research (Ofsted 2019)

'Effective questioning is one of the most widely studied aspects of teaching. We therefore have considerable evidence in this area. Teachers provide substantive feedback to pupils, resulting either from pupils' questions or from answers to teachers' questions.

Most questions can elicit correct or at least substantive answers. Correct answers need to be acknowledged in a positive but businesslike fashion. When a pupil answers a question partially correctly, the teacher can prompt that pupil to find the remaining part of the answer before moving on to the next pupil.

When a pupil answers a question incorrectly, the teacher needs to point out swiftly that the answer is wrong. If the pupil has answered incorrectly due to inattention or carelessness, the teacher can swiftly move on to the next pupil.

If the answer is incorrect due to lack of knowledge, the teacher needs to try and prompt the pupil to answer correctly. Teachers need to make sure that girls and shy pupils, who may be less assertive, have the chance to answer questions...'

Background information

Education inspection framework - Overview of research (Ofsted 2019)

'The types of questions asked are typically varied and depend on the knowledge and skills to be mastered.

The ***best strategy would appear to be to use a mixture of recall and higher-order questions***, increasing the latter as the level of understanding increases.

This does not mean that a mix should be used in all lessons; depending on where the lesson sits within a sequence of lessons about a particular topic, the balance can be strongly towards one or the other.

Teachers can use both product questions (calling for a single response from pupils) and process questions (calling for explanations from pupils). Again, the balance will depend on the lesson and topic. Pupils can be encouraged to ask questions, which can be redirected to the class before being answered by the teacher.

Relevant pupil comments can be incorporated into the lesson...'

Background information

Metacognition and self-regulation – from the EEF Teaching and Learning Toolkit

''Metacognition and self-regulation approaches aim to help pupils think about their own learning more explicitly, often by teaching them specific strategies for planning, monitoring and evaluating their learning.

Self-regulated learning can be broken into three essential components:

cognition - the mental process involved in knowing, understanding, and learning
metacognition - often defined as 'learning to learn'; and
motivation - willingness to engage our metacognitive and cognitive skills.

Metacognition and self-regulation approaches have consistently high levels of impact, with pupils making an average of seven months' additional progress.

These strategies are usually more effective when taught in collaborative groups so that learners can support each other and make their thinking explicit through discussion.'

Improving questioning in English

Improving Questioning in **English**	The Knowledge Dimension			
	Factual	**Conceptual**	**Procedural**	**Metacognitive**
Remember	Who was the author of the book? What is an adverb? Can you point to the exclamation mark? What other books are by this author? Can you recite…?	When should you begin a new paragraph in your writing? Can you think of another example of a simile? Which genre is this? What has happened in the story so far?	What do you need to remember when proof-reading your written work? How can you check it is a full sentence? Have you used 'look – cover-write-check'? What have you improved, based on the marking/feedback?	Is there a way of helping you remember the tricky spellings? Can you use an acronym or acrostic to help you? Which other books have read that had a similar theme/ style/ character? Have you written something similar before?
Understand	Why do we use this punctuation here? How do you know who spoke to the main character first? Which words give you the key information? Can you give me a definition for this word?	Why is this word / sentence so important? How do you know this a pun? What was the main idea or theme the writer is trying to convey? How do you know it is the past tense?	Why are drafting and re-drafting important? Can you summarise the plot? Can you explain your word choices to a friend? Can you identify the grammatical features of the writing?	Can you predict what will happen next in the story? Can you say / write it in your own words? What might help you to better understand this paragraph? What can you infer from the text?

Improving Questioning in **English**	The Knowledge Dimension			
	Factual	**Conceptual**	**Procedural**	**Metacognitive**
Apply	Can you change the tense? Can you group the words by their suffixes? Which words would best describe…? How do you know where to place the apostrophe?	What theme links these stories? How do you know this poem was written a long time ago? When should you begin a new paragraph? Is it similar to any other words you know?	Can you write a set of instructions for…? How do you use a dictionary? Can you re-write the complex sentence but keep the grammatical sense? How can you develop the sense of threat to your character in your writing?	What questions would you ask an author or poet? Do you need to adapt a task to fit your preferred learning style? Why do you prefer that genre? What techniques does the author use that you could 'magpie' for your own writing?
Analyse	Which events could not have happened? If this happened, how would the ending have been different? How do you know the facts are accurate? Can you distinguish between…?	Why does the rhythm of the poem change in this verse? Do these spelling rules always apply? How is this description more effective than the first? Why does the tense change?	How has the author developed the feeling of…? How has your final draft developed from your plan? Why does this method improve your spelling? Why must you be careful when applying this 'rule'?	What do you already know about this aspect of English that might be useful? When should you skim read and when should you read in detail? What are the most useful pieces of information? How would finding out more information help you?

Improving Questioning in **English**	The Knowledge Dimension			
	Factual	**Conceptual**	**Procedural**	**Metacognitive**
Evaluate	Why is that paragraph the most informative? What specific vocabulary best describes the character? Why is the account convincing? Could you improve the text, using the information you have read?	Is the account believable? What influence has the author had on other writers? What are the positive and the negative aspects of the report? How would the story look from another characters' perspective?	Why did you choose this approach? Does a story always have to start at the chronological beginning? Why is a non-chronological report the best way to present this information? Can you defend this position?	If you were learning about this aspect of English again, what would you do differently and why? What helps you learn in English and why? What do you find most difficult in English lessons and why? Which are the most useful things to remember and why?
Create	Can you produce a fact file from your research? Can you prepare a five minute presentation? How many words can you find with the same spelling pattern? Can you give the opposite view?	Can you explain spelling patterns using what you have found out about morphology and etymology? Can you use a story map / mountain to plan your work? Can you choose the best approach to present the information? How many ways can you describe the character?	If you change from the active to the passive voice what is the impact? Is it ever ok to break 'the rules' of grammar? Can you explain to a friend how you inferred the meaning from the text? How might the heroine from a different story react in this situation?	What do you want to learn in this unit of work and why is it useful? Can you select work that demonstrates your learning? Where could you apply these skills in another subject or context? How will you develop your English skills and knowledge next?

Improving questioning in maths

Improving Questioning in **Maths**	The Knowledge Dimension			
	Factual	**Conceptual**	**Procedural**	**Metacognitive**
Remember	What is this number? Is this the correct symbol? Can you identify this Roman numeral? How many times did…?	Which number comes next? What time is it? What does this digit represent? Is this a 2D or a 3D shape?	Can you order these numbers? What shape came next? How should you set out this calculation? What are the steps to solving a problem?	Can you think of a way to help you remember? Which strategy did you use? Which resources helped you to work it out? Have you used a similar method before?
Understand	How did you calculate this? Which method did you use? Why did you do it this way? Can you write this calculation in a different way?	Which clock shows the correct time? Can you identify the maths in the written problem? Can you classify these shapes? Which number/shape is the odd one out?	Can you continue the pattern or sequence? How would you explain this? What has gone wrong in this calculation? Will you have the same product if you swap the numbers?	What might help you understand this aspect of maths? Can you predict…? How does that resource help you? Why is that method the best?

Improving Questioning in **Maths**	The Knowledge Dimension			
	Factual	**Conceptual**	**Procedural**	**Metacognitive**
Apply	What mathematical rule might apply here? What do you already about your times tables that might help you? How would you describe…? What is the inverse of…	What other ways could you solve this? Can you explain to a friend how you worked it out? Why is there more than one correct answer? If you know 7 x 6 is 42, then what is 70 x 6 and 700 x 6?	How do you use a calculator with this two-step problem? Can you use the same steps as before? What calculation strategy will you use to solve this problem? Can you show me where you think you went wrong?	What have you learnt about in maths previously that might be useful in this unit of work? What strategies will you use to check your answers? What method of presenting statistics could you use to effectively compare your data? Do you need to adapt a task to fit your preferred learning style?
Analyse	Why is it correct? Could there be another outcome? How do you know the fraction is equivalent to the decimal? Is the set of numbers complete?	Can both outcomes be accurate? Do the same rules apply for all these shapes? Is the mean average more useful than mode in this instance? Could you arrive at the same destination using fewer directions?	Is there a more reliable/quicker method? Why was the answer different from your estimate? Is this method similar to another method you have used? Where did you make the mistake?	What do you already know about a different shape that might be useful? Do you know how to work through this problem? What are the most useful pieces of information? Would another example help you understand?

Improving Questioning in Maths	The Knowledge Dimension			
	Factual	**Conceptual**	**Procedural**	**Metacognitive**
Evaluate	Are your methods consistent? What are the differences between the two sets of data? Does this method work for all the calculations? Could you classify the shapes with the criteria you chose?	Are all these numbers relevant? Which estimate is likely to be most accurate? How will you use this method for measuring much larger amounts? Can you simplify the formula if you know the value of y remains constant?	Why did you choose this alternative approach? Can you explain this method of calculation? How would you work this out next time, based on what you have learned? Is there a way to improve the accuracy of your estimations?	If you were learning about this aspect of maths again, what would you do differently and why? What helps you learn in maths and why? What do you find most difficult about maths and why? Which are the most useful mathematical rules and methods to remember and why?
Create	What time does each event happen during a normal school day? Can you define this mathematical term? How many ways can you make this number? How many ways can you describe this shape?	Can you still solve the problem if you don't use addition this time? What questions could you ask to find out more information before you solve the problem? Can you decide the most appropriate intervals for the x axis and the y axis? Based on floor area, can you improve the layout of the classroom/school?	Can you create your own method to find the answer? What would happen if you changed a number/ a symbol/ the order of the calculation…? What is the minimum number of times table facts you need to know? Can you improve our class 'problem solving steps'?	What do you want to learn in this unit of work and why is it useful? Can you select work that demonstrates your learning? Can you describe what makes a really great mathematician? How will you develop your maths skills and knowledge next?

Improving questioning in science

Improving Questioning in **Science**	The Knowledge Dimension			
	Factual	**Conceptual**	**Procedural**	**Metacognitive**
Remember	What is this flower called? Can you make a list of different reptiles? What are the ends of the magnet called? Who is the naturalist in the picture?	What is a variable? What is a fossil? Which did we learn about digestion? What happened to the water?	What happened next? What are the steps we follow when carrying out an experiment? What happens to food once it is inside the mouth? Can you remember the next stage in the life cycle?	Is there a way of helping you remember each stage of the process? Can you use an acronym or acrostic to help you? What have you learned about in other science lessons that could help you? Why do scientists make notes and recordings?
Understand	Why does the plant have roots? What is the function of the liver? Can you give me a definition for this scientific word? Why must we be careful when using…?	Can you sort these flowers by size? Why were only some objects attracted to the magnet? Why didn't the feather fall straight downwards? If there were fewer rabbits, what effect would this have on the food chain?	Why should you only change one variable in the experiment? Why is it important to repeat experiments? Can you explain why the days are shorter in winter in this country? How is sedimentary rock formed?	Can you predict the results of the experiment? Why do you think this happened? Can you explain the findings in your own words? What might help you to better understand the movements of the moon and Earth?

Improving Questioning in **Science**	The Knowledge Dimension			
	Factual	**Conceptual**	**Procedural**	**Metacognitive**
Apply	What do you already know about this plant? Using your research, how can you group the animals? Which scientific words would best describe…? Which observations prove that?	Are there any similarities between…? Can you think of another process like this? When does digestion begin and when does it end? Can you give some advice to the other group?	How do you carry out a fair test? How do you use this equipment accurately? What safety rules do you need to follow? How will you plot the data?	What questions would you ask a scientist? Do you need to adapt a task to fit your preferred learning style? How are you being a scientist? What scientific methods and techniques did you use?
Analyse	What do your results tell you? Were your predictions accurate? How did you check your facts? Did any results surprise you? If so, why?	Why do the rocks have different properties? Which of our 'healthy lifestyle' timetables would you recommend and why? Why was this experiment more reliable? Why did the cress grow better in that location?	What do you think went wrong? Can you explain what must have happened when…? How did that famous scientist carry out their work? What caused the change to occur?	What do you already know about this aspect of science that might be useful? What are the most useful pieces of information? How would finding out more information help you? What motivated the person to become a scientist?

Improving Questioning in **Science**	The Knowledge Dimension			
	Factual	**Conceptual**	**Procedural**	**Metacognitive**
Evaluate	Why is that website a reliable source of scientific information? What specific scientific vocabulary best describes this? Why are your results accurate? What information or data is missing?	What influence has that scientist / naturalist had? What are the positive and the negative aspects of selective breeding in dogs? Why is that scientific knowledge of value? Are all the results of the experiment relevant?	Why did you choose this approach? Was this the most reliable way to test your hypothesis? Why is it difficult to replicate some experiments? How would you defend Darwin and Wallace against their critics?	If you were learning about this aspect of science again, what would you do differently and why? What helps you learn in science and why? What do you find most difficult in science lessons and why? Which are the most useful things to remember and why?
Create	Can you prepare an assembly about the importance of cleaning our teeth? Can you produce a ppt about amphibians? Can you provide illustrations for each season of the year? How many objects can you find made of that material?	Who could help you carry out this investigation? How will you convince me the test was fair? Can you compare the data in more than one way? Can you create and illustrate your own scale to measure wind strength?	Can you produce a 'Guide to Carrying Out Experiments' for the younger children? During the day, can you prove the Earth is rotating on its axis by using webcams from around the world's cities? Can you explain the process to a friend? What could change the results of the test and why?	What do you want to learn in this unit of work and why is it useful? Can you select work that demonstrates your learning? How might this scientific knowledge be useful in other subjects? How will you develop your science skills and knowledge next?

Improving questioning in geography

Improving Questioning in **Geography**	The Knowledge Dimension			
	Factual	**Conceptual**	**Procedural**	**Metacognitive**
Remember	Can you name the capital city of…? Which rivers can you name in the USA? Can you identify the mountain shown on the map? Where on the globe are North America and South America?	Why does deforestation occur? How is a beach formed? What direction is the nearest (name a feature or settlement) from the school? How far is the place we visited on a field trip from here?	Can you describe your journey? What were the stages of settlement? How was the fuel transported from A to B? What happened after the boat passed that part of the river?	Can you think of a way to help you remember the directions of the compass? Should you draw, write or photograph your findings and which is best? How will you remember the continents on a globe or map? Can you think of an acrostic to help you remember the place names?
Understand	What are the differences between a village, a town and a city? How do you know this picture shows a port? What does this symbol represent on the OS map? What is a biome?	What are the equator and the Tropics of Cancer and Capricorn? Why do we have time zones? Why might people move to live in a city? What are contour lines on a map?	How did the village develop into a town? How is a volcano formed? Can you describe the route shown on the map? How does water from the top of a mountain reach the sea?	What might help you understand this aspect of geography? Can you predict the next stage of the journey? Can you use the map key yourself? Do you prefer to use books or the internet to help you find the answer?

Improving Questioning in **Geography**	The Knowledge Dimension			
	Factual	**Conceptual**	**Procedural**	**Metacognitive**
Apply	What do you already know about this place? How would you describe…? Can you use these geographical words in a sentence? Which of these words are associated with mountains?	What other ways could you get to school? Can you show me the location using a six-figure grid reference? Can you explain to a friend why the weather is hotter in this place? Why are there few forests in the UK?	How do you use an atlas? Can you carry out a fieldwork task as explained? Can you write a set of instructions for using a compass? What questions would you ask a polar explorer?	What have you learnt about in geography previously that might be useful in this unit of work? What research strategies would you use to find out more about the oceans? What maths skills and knowledge could you use to best present your fieldwork data? Do you need to adapt a task to fit your preferred learning style?
Analyse	Do more people live in place A, B or C? Which type of energy does each country use most of? What proportion of the country is cultivated land? Which is the most complete list of features that describe the place?	Can you compare life in a seaside town with life in a farming village? Can you explain the areas shown in the aerial photograph? Why might car journeys take longer in the future? Why do people live in earthquake zones?	What does our fieldwork data tell us? How do humans impact on this area? How does the physical location influence where people live? How do we know if the information on a website is reliable?	What do you already know about a different place that might be relevant? How will you know the field work data is accurate? What are the most useful pieces of information? Would a different example to help you understand?

Improving Questioning in **Geography**	The Knowledge Dimension			
	Factual	**Conceptual**	**Procedural**	**Metacognitive**
Evaluate	Which statements best describe this particular river? What are the main differences between England and a named non-European country? Which map is most accurate and up to date? Which guidebook provides the most useful information about the town?	Would you prefer to life in Place A or Place B? Why wouldn't a meercat like to live at the North Pole? Can you list the positive and the negative aspects of air travel? How does climate impact on settlement patterns?	Is a digital map always more useful than a paper map when going on a journey? Should we try to stop coastal erosion? What are the realistic alternatives to the existing land use in a specific area? What is the best source of geographical information for this task?	What are your top three tips for someone who wants to find out about the place we have been studying? If you were learning about this aspect of geography again, what would you do differently and why? What helps you learn in geography and why? What do you find most difficult about geography and why?
Create	What are the best features of our town? What facts would you include in a fact file about a non-European country? Can you describe the ideal place for the headteacher to live? Can you produce a glossary of geographical terms?	Can you identify the human geographical features of a region or area? How would you classify these geographical terms? Can you create your own classification for wind measurement? Why are imports and exports important?	How could you record and compare the daily findings from our weather station? Can you plan a stage-by-stage journey from our school to…? How can we reduce global warming? What might this country look like in 1000 years because of geographical processes?	What do you want to learn in this unit of work and why? Can you select work to include in our floorbook that demonstrates your learning? Can you describe what makes a really great geographer? How will you develop your geographical skills in the future?

Improving questioning in history

Improving Questioning in **History**	The Knowledge Dimension			
	Factual	**Conceptual**	**Procedural**	**Metacognitive**
Remember	Can you name this Roman leader? Can you identify the person shown in this old photograph? When did this event take place? What did people have to eat then?	Was this event before or after the voyage of Columbus? How long ago was Skara Brae a settlement? Which peoples have invaded Britain? Is this primary or secondary historical source?	Can you put this event on the timeline? How can you check historical facts? What happened after the event? Can you put these invaders in chronological order from earliest to most recent?	Can you think of a way to help you remember the dates? Should you draw, write or photograph your findings and which is best? How will you remember the suffixes that identify Viking settlements? Can you think of an acrostic to help you remember the sequence of events?
Understand	Can you summarize the main differences between two events or periods? How do you know this picture is old? Why are there no You Tube clips from this period? Why did Rosa Parks not move on the bus?	What is parliament? Why are Columbus and Neil Armstrong similar? What can we learn from archaeologists? Can you classify these historical sources?	Why is it important to use a range of source material? How do you access online census archives for our area? Can you describe the journey Florence Nightingale took to the Crimea? Why did invaders begin to settle?	What might help you understand this aspect of History? Can you predict what happened next? Can you use the online resource yourself? Do you prefer to use books or the internet to help you find the information?

Improving Questioning in **History**	**The Knowledge Dimension**			
	Factual	**Conceptual**	**Procedural**	**Metacognitive**
Apply	What do you already know about this period in time? How would you describe…? Can you use these historical words in a sentence? Which of these words are associated with the Romans?	What other ways could you find information? Can you show me the information about the household at one address? Can you explain to a friend why the settlement was built at that location? Why are there few Viking place names in the south of the country?	How do you use a historical atlas? Can you carry out a research as explained? Can you write a set of instructions for using the school library's History section? How would a historian approach this?	What have you learnt about in History previously that might be useful in this unit of work? What research strategies would you use to find out more about this person? What writing skills and knowledge could you use to best present your research? Do you need to adapt a task to fit your preferred learning style?
Analyse	Which civilisation lasted the longest? Which weapons were most effective? Which laws do we still have today? Which is the most complete list of artefacts from that time?	Can you compare life in a Roman town with life in a modern town? Can you explain the tools shown in the early photograph? Which events could not have happened? Why did the changes occur?	What were the motives behind…? What was the turning point in this sequence of events? What influenced the person to do this? How do we know if the information on a website is reliable?	What do you already know about a different period that might be relevant? How will you know the source material is relevant to this time? What are the most useful pieces of information? Would a different example to help you understand?

Improving Questioning in **History**	The Knowledge Dimension			
	Factual	**Conceptual**	**Procedural**	**Metacognitive**
Evaluate	Which statements best describe this person? What are the main differences between William Caxton and Tim Berners-Lee? Which account is likely to be most accurate? Which source provides the most useful information?	When would you have preferred to live? Could they have made a different decision? What influence do the Romans still have on our lives? How did the first railways make a difference to our town?	What were the consequences of this event or decision? Who gained and who lost when this happened? What were the realistic alternatives for this person at that time? What is the best source of historical information for this task?	What are your top three tips for someone who wants to find out about the period we have been studying? If you were learning about this aspect of History again, what would you do differently and why? What helps you learn in History and why? What do you find most difficult about History and why?
Create	Can you describe a day in the life of…? What facts would you include in a fact file about a famous historical figure? Can you describe what the village would have looked and sounded like then? Can you define this historical term?	Can you identify the human geographical features of a region or area? How would you classify these historical artefacts? Can you create your own set of questions based on what you have already found out about this person? What questions could you ask to find out more about this artefact?	What might have happened if Harold had fought the Normans first, and then fought the Vikings? Can you create your own time line of events? With hindsight, can you see a possible solution to their problem? Can you continue their story?	What do you want to learn in this unit of work and why? Can you select work to include in our floorbook that demonstrates your learning? Can you describe what makes a really great historian? How will you develop your historical skills in the future?

Improving questioning in
art

Improving Questioning in **Art**	The Knowledge Dimension			
	Factual	**Conceptual**	**Procedural**	**Metacognitive**
Remember	Which artist painted this picture? Can you identify this artist? What colour is this? Which are the primary colours?	Which colours will you mix to make brown? What does texture mean? What is painting in this style called? What tools do we use to shape the clay?	What do you need to remember when working with clay? How did you create that effect? What are the steps to developing the layers? What process did that artist use?	How does your sketch book help you? Which methods did you use? Which resources helped you create the final art work? Have you used similar methods before?
Understand	Which technique did you use? Why did you do it this way? Why did the artist choose this?	Can you classify these objects? Which of these pictures are examples of Pop Art? What was the main idea or theme the artists was trying to convey? Which picture is the odd one out?	How will you produce this effect? What steps will you follow to make this? Can you explain the process to a friend? Can you show me what I did when I showed you how to make the clay pot?	What might help you understand this aspect of art? Can you predict what will happen if…? How does that resource help you? Why is that technique important?

Improving Questioning in Art	The Knowledge Dimension			
	Factual	**Conceptual**	**Procedural**	**Metacognitive**
Apply	What do we know about the media we are using that will be useful? What do you already about colour mixing that might help you? How would you describe…? What is same as the last piece of art you produced?	What theme links these examples of art? How could you create a 3D effect here? How might these two different media be used together? How is this typical of art in this style/period?	How do you use this tool in this situation? Can you use the same steps as before? What technique/s will you use to develop your final piece? How can you develop the range of colours on the palate?	What questions would you ask the artist? What techniques will you use to improve your work? How will you present your final piece? Do you need to adapt a task to fit your preferred learning style?
Analyse	How is your picture typical of this style? Could there be another outcome? How do you know the picture is probably by the same artist? Why did the artist change style?	How is this…similar to…? How do you distinguish between this piece and the other piece? How is this technique more effective than the first method you tried? Could you arrive at the same destination using fewer directions?	Is there a more effective process? How has the final piece developed from your sketches? Can you explain what must have happened when…? If the process was different, what might be the impact?	What do you already know about this aspect of art that might be useful? Do you know how to work through this process? What are the most useful pieces of information? How would seeing more examples of art from this period or style help you?

Improving Questioning in **Art**	The Knowledge Dimension			
	Factual	**Conceptual**	**Procedural**	**Metacognitive**
Evaluate	Why is that section of your picture most realistic? What specific art vocabulary best describes the differences between the two pieces? Why does the 'dry brush' technique work in this style of picture? Could you classify the artworks using your own criteria, using the vocabulary we have learned?	Why do you prefer the work of this artist? What influence has … had on art? Is graffiti always a good or a bad thing? What do you think about abstract art?	Why did you choose this alternative approach? Can you explain the benefits of this technique? How would you complete this artwork next time, based on what you have learned? Can you simplify the technique or process?	If you were learning about this aspect of art again, what would you do differently and why? What helps you learn in art and why? What do you find most difficult in art lessons and why? Which are the most useful artistic techniques and knowledge to remember and why?
Create	Can you show how landscape art has developed using a time line? How do you define this artistic term? How many different emotions can you show using this method? Where does the frame give the best view?	If you could use any media, why would you choose…? Can you create a new version of this work? Can you decide which is the most contrasting pattern? How can you improve the effect to draw the viewers' eyes to the main feature of the picture?	Can you devise your own way to…? What would happen if you changed…? How many ways could you add texture to your work? Can you improve the process to develop light and shade in the piece?	What do you want to learn in this unit of work and why is it useful? Can you select work that demonstrates your learning? Can you describe what makes a really great artist? How will you develop your art skills and knowledge next?

Improving questioning in

music

Improving Questioning in **Music**	**The Knowledge Dimension**			
	Factual	**Conceptual**	**Procedural**	**Metacognitive**
Remember	What is this instrument called? What song did we sing? Which sound file do you need? Which note is that?	How do we warm up our voices? How do we hold this instrument? What part are you singing within the class performance? What is a flat or sharp note?	Can you identify the chorus and verses? Which technique will you use to play this instrument? Can you sing the melody? What comes next in the music?	What are the key points to practice? How will you remember this next time? What have you learned about in other music lessons and activities that could help you now? What musical skills and knowledge do you already have?
Understand	What is this instrument used for? What does that notation mean? What part does that instrument play? What is tempo?	Why do we warm up our voices? Why is it played in that why? Why are the pauses important? Can you classify these instruments?	How do you know when to start and when to stop playing? Why does the music increase in volume at this point? What are the basic techniques for playing? How did this style of music develop?	Why do you enjoy that music in particular? Can you explain what you have learned in your own words? What might help you to develop your playing technique? Which aspect of singing do you want to improve?

Improving Questioning in **Music**	The Knowledge Dimension			
	Factual	**Conceptual**	**Procedural**	**Metacognitive**
Apply	How is the instrument used in different styles of music? What do you already know about composers? How does this sound similar to…? Why would this particular instrument be a good choice?	How have you used a particular musical skill? Can you offer advice based on what you have learned so far about this song? What will help your group work collaboratively on this musical task? Why do those sounds / instruments work well together?	Why did you choose this sound within your composition? Can you teach another child how to play / sing that part? What can you tell me about this style of music? How is the musician achieving that sound?	What questions would you ask a professional musician? What musical skills and knowledge did you choose to use? What techniques did you improve? Which aspects of music could you develop further?
Analyse	What is different about this musical style? Which instruments / voices could you hear? Can you order the string instruments by size? What caused it to go out of tune?	Can you think of another song where this style could be appropriate? What are the differences between the violin and cello? What are some of the difficulties in using this instrument? When can you hear the lowest / highest notes?	Where did you make the mistake? How might breaking the song down into smaller steps help? Can you explain how to use the instrument? What did you choose to rehearse?	What do you already know about this aspect of music that might be useful? Which can you play particularly well? What should you focus on in practice? What are your musical strengths and what are the areas to develop further?

Improving Questioning in **Music**	The Knowledge Dimension			
	Factual	**Conceptual**	**Procedural**	**Metacognitive**
Evaluate	Which song do you prefer singing and why? Which instrument did you play particularly well? What did you hear that you liked best? Which technique enable you to control the sound most effectively?	Why do these songs make you feel happy / sad? Which musical techniques work best? How do you know you played the song well? What changes would you recommend to improve the performance?	Which aspect of the musical performance / song are you best at? Why this is the most complicated part of the song? Do you achieve the mood you wanted in the music? How did that musician / band have a lasting influence?	If you were learning about this aspect of music again, what would you do differently and why? What helps you learn in music and why? Which techniques do you think are most useful and why? Which are the most useful musical skills and knowledge you have acquired and why?
Create	Can you create your own notation to record your composition? Can you tell the story of a famous musician? How would you define that style of music? Why should people come and see your group perform their composition?	Who will you choose to work with collaboratively on this composition, based on their skills and knowledge? How can you better contribute to the group? What would happen if you used different instruments? How many ways could you develop that opening piece?	Can you explain to another child how to play the instrument? Can you explain how you have improved your performance over time? How could you incorporate other styles into the composition? Can you give creative feedback on that music, like a helpful judge on a talent show?	What do you want to learn in this unit of work and why is it useful? Can you select work that demonstrates your learning? What links can you make between music and science, history, English and maths? How will you develop your musical skills and knowledge next?

Improving questioning in

technology

Improving Questioning in **Design Technology**	The Knowledge Dimension			
	Factual	**Conceptual**	**Procedural**	**Metacognitive**
Remember	What ingredients did you use? What fabric is this? Who is this designer? What is the tool called?	Can you name some healthy foods? How did you reinforce the structure? What did you learn about diet? What happened to the prototype?	What happened next? What are the steps we follow designing and making a product? How do you use this tool safely? Can you remember the next stage in the design process?	What are your design criteria? Is there a way of helping you remember each stage of the design process? What have you learned about in other DT lessons that could help you? What construction skills do you already have?
Understand	What does a pulley used for? What is the function of the gears? Can you give me a definition of 'flexible'? How does the computer control the device?	Why did we design and make a prototype first? Why did you reinforce the structure? How can you strengthen the join? What do we mean applying 'finish' to the product?	What are the stages in the design process? What are the stages in the production process? Why do we develop a prototype before the final product? Why is it important to use tools carefully?	Why do designers often try different versions before choosing one? Why do you think this is the best option? Can you explain the design in your own words? What might help you to better understand the way pulleys work?

Improving Questioning in **Design Technology**	The Knowledge Dimension			
	Factual	**Conceptual**	**Procedural**	**Metacognitive**
Apply	How is the product used? What do you already know about this component or device? How have you met the design criteria? Which technical words would best describe the working of the mechanism?	Are there any similarities between the two materials? How could you use electrical components in your design to make it 'hands free'? What factors would you change in the next stage of the design process? Can you offer advice based on your own work?	How will you develop your prototype? How do you use this tool with this material? What safety rules do you need to follow? How will you record the feedback you receive about your design?	What questions would you ask a designer? How might a famous designer approach this design brief? Do you need to adapt a task to fit your preferred learning style? What technological methods and techniques did you use?
Analyse	What do your testing of the prototype tell you? What did you learn from feedback about your product? How local are the ingredients you have chosen? Are there similar products already available?	Can you think of another instance where this product could be useful? What makes your design distinctive and different? How is it functional / practical? How would it be marketed as a saleable product?	Which step of the production process will you have to improve? Can you explain what must have happened when…? Can you explain how to use all the components in the kit? How could you change how the cam moves without changing the whole structure?	What do you already know about this aspect of DT that might be useful? Which tools can you use particularly well? How would finding out more information help you? Does everyone share your opinion about your product?

Improving Questioning in **Design Technology**	**The Knowledge Dimension**			
	Factual	**Conceptual**	**Procedural**	**Metacognitive**
Evaluate	How does the product meet the design brief? What technical vocabulary best describes this? Which menu is the healthiest? What materials have the best properties for the task?	What are the positive and the negative aspects of the design? Why is that element of the structure so crucial? What elements would you copy from existing products? How has that designer influenced us?	Why did you choose this approach to construct your product? How will you evaluate your ideas? How will you gather the views of other people about your design? If you built it again, what would you change?	If you were learning about this aspect of DT again, what would you do differently and why? What helps you learn in DT and why? What do you find most difficult in DT lessons and why? Which are the most useful techniques to remember and why?
Create	Can you develop an advert promoting your product? Can you prove you have met and even exceeded the design brief? Can you list the benefits of your design or meal? How many ways could the product be used?	How could you combine elements of both designs? How will you convince someone your design is best? How could you show the nutritional benefits of your chosen recipe? Where will you find the expert knowledge you need?	Could you make an instruction or recipe booklet on how to make your product? Can you explain to the class the process you went through to arrive at your final design? Could you devise your own way to make it work? How could the process be more efficient?	What do you want to learn in this unit of work and why is it useful? Can you select work that demonstrates your learning? What links can you make between DT and science, English, art, computing or maths? How will you develop your DT skills and knowledge next?

Improving questioning in computing

Improving Questioning in **Computing**	The Knowledge Dimension			
	Factual	**Conceptual**	**Procedural**	**Metacognitive**
Remember	What is that part of the computer called? What software is this? What is that icon? What is that device used for?	Can you name other programs you have used? How did you use the software? What did we learn about debugging? What was the problem that we are using the program to solve?	What happened next? Can you describe the algorithm? What must you remember to make sure you stay safe online? Can you remember the next stage in the programming process?	What do you need to save and what will you remember yourself? How will you remember this next time? What have you learned about in other computing work that could help you? What computing skills do you already have?
Understand	What is this software used for? Where is the information stored? Can you give me a definition of 'streaming'? Where is this technology used?	How does the computer control the device? Why did you choose this step in the code? What is the difference between the internet and the world wide web? What do we mean by sequence when we code?	What are the steps for embedding a video clip into the presentation? How do you check the code for errors? Why is it important to use digital technology carefully? What are the instructions for using this device?	Why do you think this is the best way to…? Can you explain what the program does in your own words? What might help you to better understand the way the network works? Which digital devices do you not yet understand?

Improving Questioning in **Computing**	The Knowledge Dimension			
	Factual	**Conceptual**	**Procedural**	**Metacognitive**
Apply	How is the software used? What do you already know about this program or device? How have you organised the information? Which search term worked?	How have you used a logical approach? Can you offer advice based on what you have learned so far about this device? How can you alter the input and output? How can you use the internet to work collaboratively?	How do you use these two devices together? What safety rules do you need to follow? How will you store the data and add more information over time? How do you make sure to can access this online on different devices?	What questions would you ask a computer technician? Do you need to adapt a task to fit your preferred learning style? What computing skills did you choose to use? How do you use digital devices in everyday life?
Analyse	How can you check the information on the website is accurate and factual? What does your testing of the coding tell you? Why did the device do that? What are the features of the software?	Can you think of another instance where this device could be useful? How is this software similar to the open source version? What information is private and personal? What are some of the problems in using this device?	How could you sharpen the search criteria? How did you debug effectively? Can you explain how to use the devices? Why did the changes in output occur?	What do you already know about this aspect of computing that might be useful? Which software can you use particularly well? How would finding out more information help you? Is using a digital device always the best option?

Improving Questioning in **Computing**	The Knowledge Dimension			
	Factual	**Conceptual**	**Procedural**	**Metacognitive**
Evaluate	What criteria will you use to evaluate your work? What technical vocabulary best describes this? Which software has the most useful features? Which device was most accurate?	How here you able to manipulate the content to suit the outcome? Can you devise your own way to achieve the same outcome? How relevant is that function? What changes would you recommend to improve the sorting of the information?	Which program worked most efficiently? Which devices enabled you to produce the interactive presentation of your work? Can you explain why this is a better solution to the problem? Which search engine is best and why?	If you were learning about this aspect of computing again, what would you do differently and why? What helps you learn in computing and why? Which digital devices do you think are most useful and why? Which are the most useful computing skills you have acquired and why?
Create	Why is your app so useful? Can you create a simple program? Can you generate a data log over time? Can you create your own digital content?	How could you combine elements from all three types of software? Who will you choose to work with collaboratively online, based on their skills and knowledge? How can you use digital technology to present the data? How can you contribute to the project?	Can you explain to another child how to use this device? Can you explain to the class the program you developed? Can you devise your own algorithm? How could the process be more efficient?	What do you want to learn in this unit of work and why is it useful? Can you select work that demonstrates your learning? What links can you make between computing and science, DT and maths? How will you develop your computing skills and knowledge next?

Improving questioning in

PE

Improving Questioning in PE	The Knowledge Dimension			
	Factual	**Conceptual**	**Procedural**	**Metacognitive**
Remember	What is this equipment called? What game did we play? What kit do you need? Which swimming stroke is that?	How many more runs did you score this lesson than last lesson? How do you know you have warmed-up? Who are the defenders and who are the attackers? What position are you playing?	What are the rules? Which techniques will you use in this gymnastics lesson? What are the safety rules with this equipment? Can you remember the steps and moves in the dance sequence?	What are the key points to remember and practice? How will you remember this next time? What have you learned about in other PE lessons and activities that could help you now? What PE skills do you already have?
Understand	What is this equipment used for? What do the markings on the court / pitch mean? Can you summarize the rules? What signals does the referee use?	Why is warming-up and cooling down important? What do we mean when we say the ball has to be passed backwards in rugby? What do we mean by a sequence of moves? Can you explain when a player is offside?	What are the sequence of moves in your dance? Do you understand why the referee blew the whistle? Why should you shower before and after swimming? Can you explain how the bowl over-arm in cricket?	Why do you think this is the best way to…? Can you explain what you have learned in your own words? What might help you to better understand the rules of the game? Which aspect of gymnastics do you want to improve now?

Improving Questioning in PE	The Knowledge Dimension			
	Factual	**Conceptual**	**Procedural**	**Metacognitive**
Apply	How is the piece of equipment used? What do you already know about this game or sport? How have you organised your team? Which tactic worked?	How have you used a particular skill? Can you offer advice based on what you have learned so far about this game? How could you organise your team to be more effective? What will help your group work collaboratively on this (outdoor and adventurous) task?	How do you work with your partner in this dance? What safety rules do you need to follow? What are the instructions for using this apparatus? In an emergency in water, how do you perform a self-rescue?	What questions would you ask a professional sportsperson? What PE skills did you choose to use? How do you lead a healthy lifestyle? Which aspects of PE could you develop further?
Analyse	Did you improve on your personal best? How did your performance improve? Why did your team perform well? Which apparatus did you feel you used particularly well?	Can you think of another sport where this skill could be useful? What are the differences between netball and basketball? Which tactics work best? What are some of the difficulties in using this apparatus?	Where did you make the mistake? How might breaking the sequence down into smaller steps help? Can you explain how to use the apparatus? Why did the team perform better in the second half?	What do you already know about this aspect of PE that might be useful? Which equipment can you use particularly well? What should you focus on in practice? What are your strengths and what are the areas to develop further?

Improving Questioning in PE	The Knowledge Dimension			
	Factual	**Conceptual**	**Procedural**	**Metacognitive**
Evaluate	What criteria will you use to evaluate your performance? How can you best describe the bowling action? Which technique enable you to control the ball most effectively? Which swimming stroke do you prefer and why?	Which activity is better for a healthy lifestyle? Is this technique useful in a real game? What changes would you recommend to improve performance?	How consistent are your performances? Which aspect of the game are you best at? Why this is the most complicated part of the sequence? What can you do to hopefully avoid strains and injuries?	If you were learning about this aspect of PE again, what would you do differently and why? What helps you learn in PE and why? Which techniques do you think are most useful and why? Which are the most useful PE skills you have acquired and why?
Create	How will you record your fitness activities over the course of a week? How could you track improvements in your performance? Can you describe the most important attributes of a team player? Which facts might convince the headteacher to organise more sports activities?	Who will you choose to work with collaboratively on this activity, based on their skills and knowledge? How can you better contribute to the team? What would happen if you used different equipment / apparatus? How many ways could you develop that movement?	Can you explain to another child how to use this equipment? Can you develop your own rules for a ball game? Can you explain how you have improved your performance over time? How could you lead an even healthier lifestyle over the next year?	What do you want to learn in this unit of work and why is it useful? Can you select work that demonstrates your learning? What links can you make between PE and science, English and maths? How will you develop your PE skills and knowledge next?

Are you looking to publish your own work?

Focus Education is an independent publisher looking to work with authors of teacher resources in primary schools. With over 25 years experience and an excellent reputation in the primary education market, we can publish and retail your work providing a full wrap around service from order to dispatch.

Advantages of publishing with Focus Education:

- Quick Turnaround
- No unnecessary red tape or administration
- Full editing, formatting & design process
- Competitive royalty rates per sale
- Full order, sale and dispatch service

For more information, please email claire@focus-education.co.uk

What do you think?

We love to hear your feedback on our products and services

Tweet Us

@focuseducation1